Vlad

and the
Roman Triumph

Kate and Sam Cunningham

We were living a life of luxury in Egypt, with Queen Cleopatra and her twin children. But that all came to a sudden end when she was defeated by the Romans and we were captured. Now we are learning Latin ready for our new life in Rome.

Even though we lost the war, they arranged this big parade and celebration for us. I thought Rome would be a bit dull, but it is going to be an amazing Triumph. Even the Emperor Augustus is here to see us.

The procession started at the Temple of the Egyptian Goddess Isis, at the city gates.

The troops let the twins, Cleopatra Selene and her brother Alexander Helios, pray before the long walk.

We only slipped away for a minute.

By the time we looked back, the procession had moved on and the twins were gone.

Felix let out an enormous wail as we watched the tail of the last crocodile flick around the corner.

Before we had a chance to chase them, we were gathered up by a child who stuffed us into their tunic.

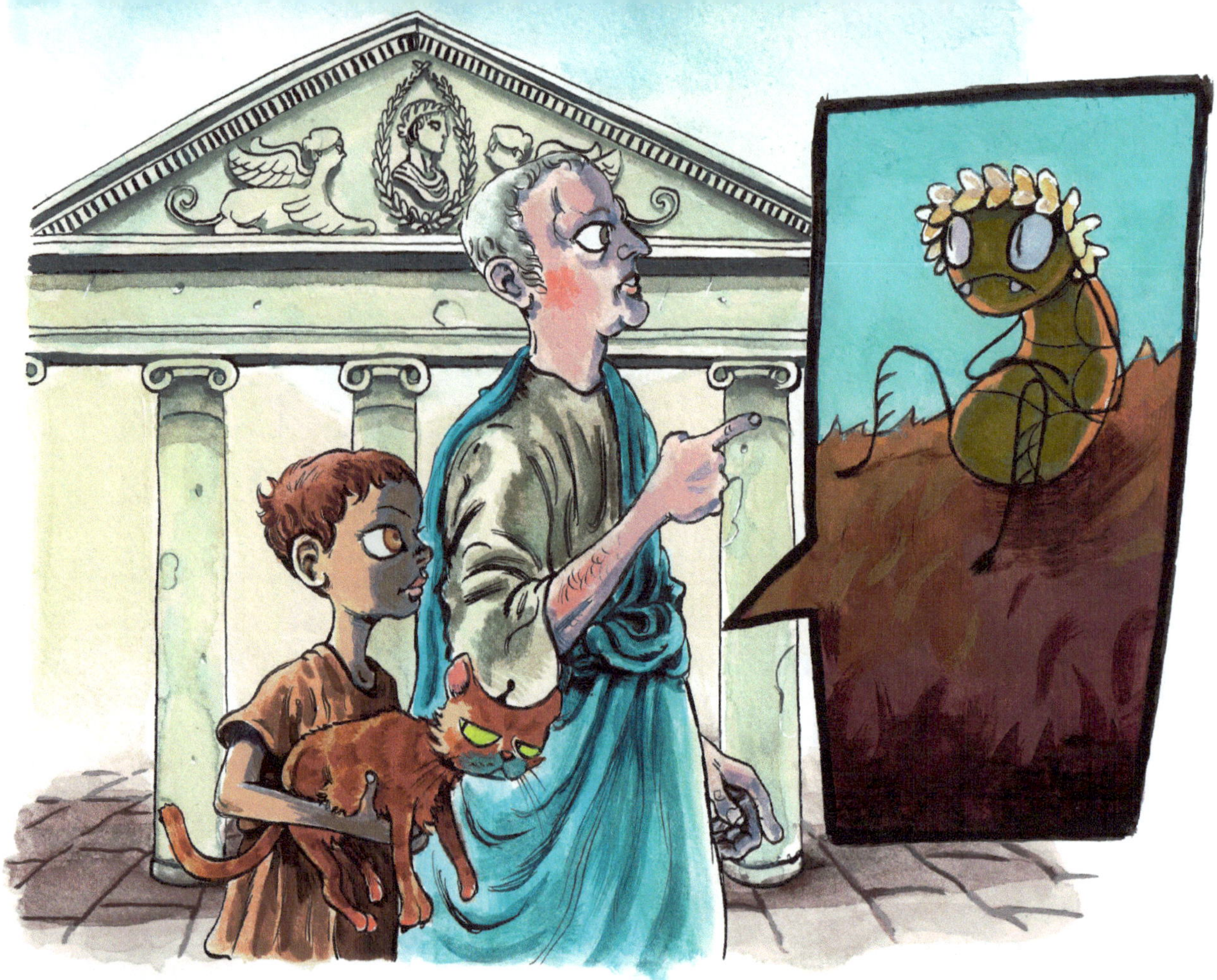

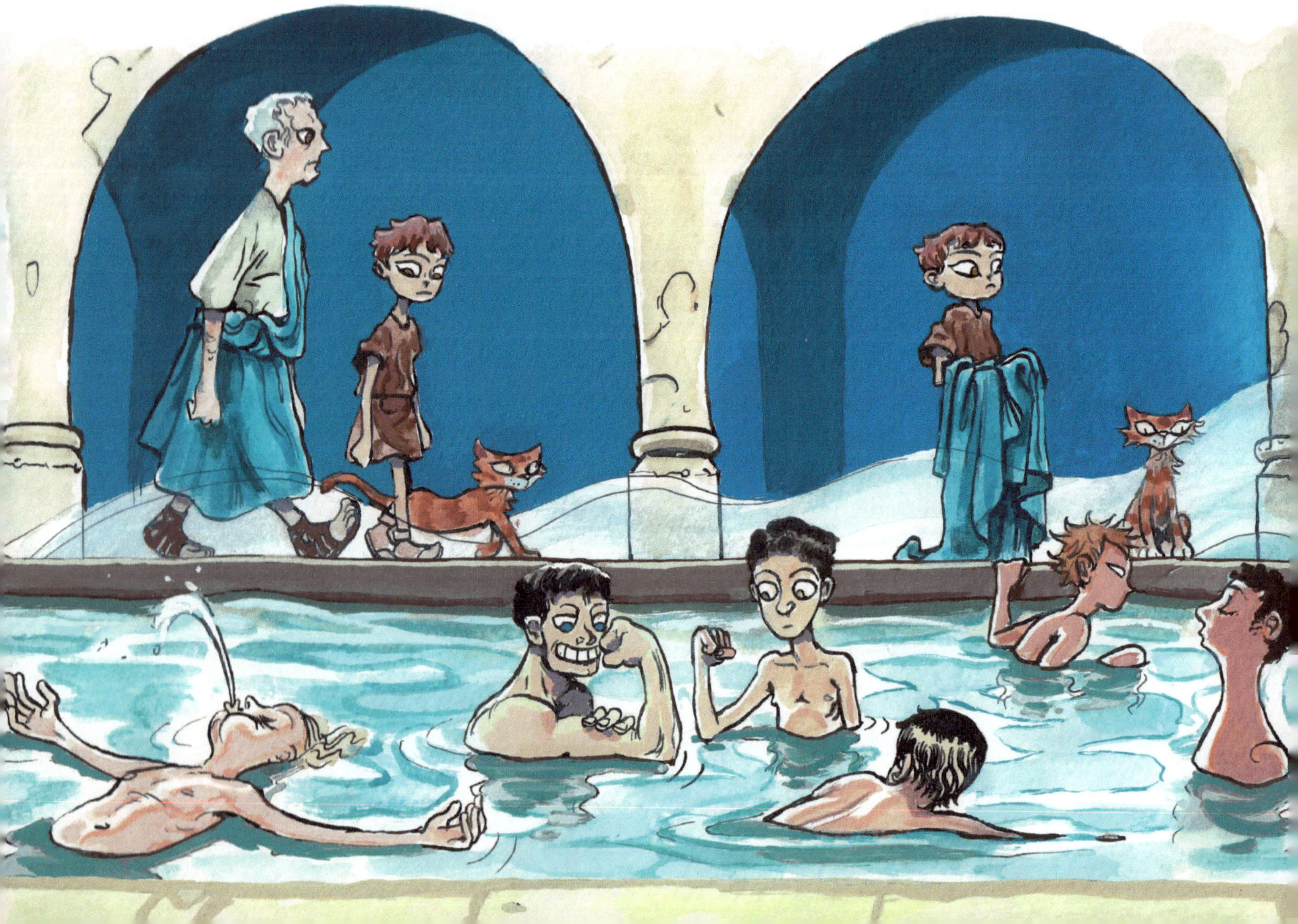

The sound of marching echoed away as our new friend trotted behind a man dressed in the sheet so many Roman men wear.

"Hurry, Blastus. We need to get to the baths before we join the end of the Triumph."

BATH! We don't like baths. We wanted to find the twins, not be forced to wash.

As we entered, the heat engulfed us immediately. It was the first time I had been warm since being taken from Egypt. Perhaps baths in Rome were not such a bad thing.

"Don't drop this toga," the man instructed, as he draped it over Blastus' arms.

The second room was even better than the first and was as hot as a cauldron. The other one now seemed tepid.

We were looking forward to the final area, but we were in for a horrible shock. I have never felt such freezing cold in my life.

After that the Roman sun seemed wonderfully warm as we stepped back out and headed down the hill.

A wave of smells filled the air and swept over us. Felix jumped up and narrowly avoided falling into a huge bowl of bubbling stew. The woman behind the counter shouted and lunged forward, but Blastus hauled us to safety.

The young slave looked longingly at the food and we could feel the rumbles of his stomach. "Can we have something to eat?" he asked timidly.

"No time." His master replied curtly. "We can't be late. Besides," he added, "don't you want to see the Manticore skeleton? It's one of the amazing treasures they discovered in Egypt."

The boy nodded miserably.

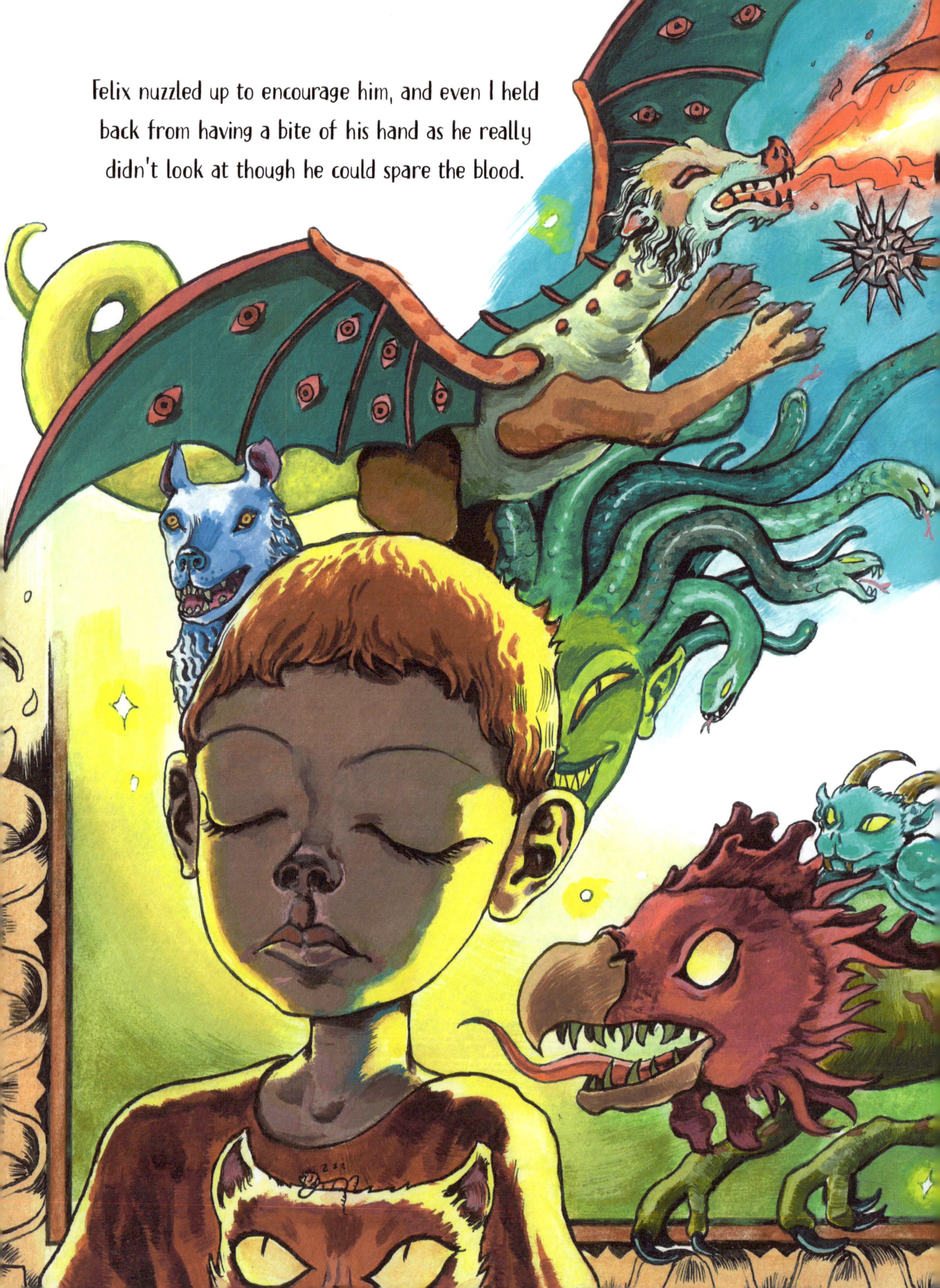

Felix nuzzled up to encourage him, and even I held back from having a bite of his hand as he really didn't look at though he could spare the blood.

We trudged on, stopping to let Blastus have a wee in a laundry vat, which apparently is acceptable in Rome. This cheered me up enormously, as I hate wasting time searching for toilets.

Ahead of us we could hear cheering and the streets were filling with crowds of people, all surging in the same direction.

We funnelled through an arch and came out into a vast arena. The troops were lined up and the whole scene seemed to glow as the sun reflected off the golden treasure piled high in carts. It was a magnificent sight, but also sad to think it had all been plundered from our homeland.

Animals were growing restless in their cages, and the slaves looked weary after marching through the streets, especially those weighed down with heavy chains.

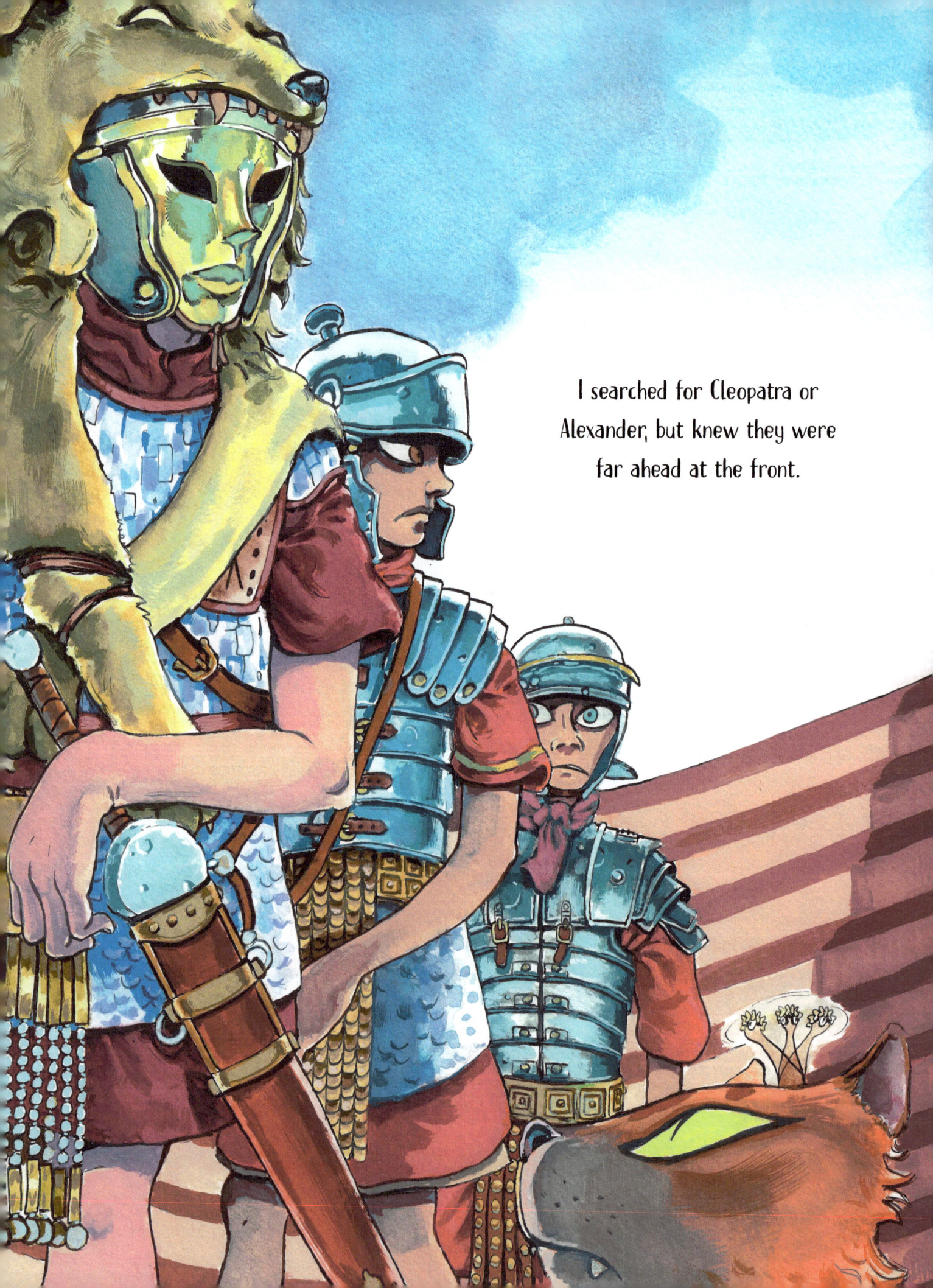
I searched for Cleopatra or Alexander, but knew they were far ahead at the front.

"Can we go and see the Manticore before we sit?" Blastus asked, and his master nodded in a way that suggested that he wanted a good look as well, but was too proud to admit it. We approached the enormous skeleton of the beast mounted high on a plinth, shuddering to imagine what it would look like in real life.

As we got near, we heard the angry barks of a canine as it pulled away from its owner, who let go of the rope.

The horses reared up and carts overturned.

Felix yowled in terror, leapt from Blastus' arms and scampered off into the crowd.

A big, hairy soldier jumped backwards into the path of his comrades, who toppled and fell on one another with a clatter.

The Manticore's bones swayed, before finally collapsing onto the ground.

Peeping out we saw that the bones had fallen to form the jumbled skeleton of the most bizarre creature. It looked more like the thrashing crocodiles in the cages.

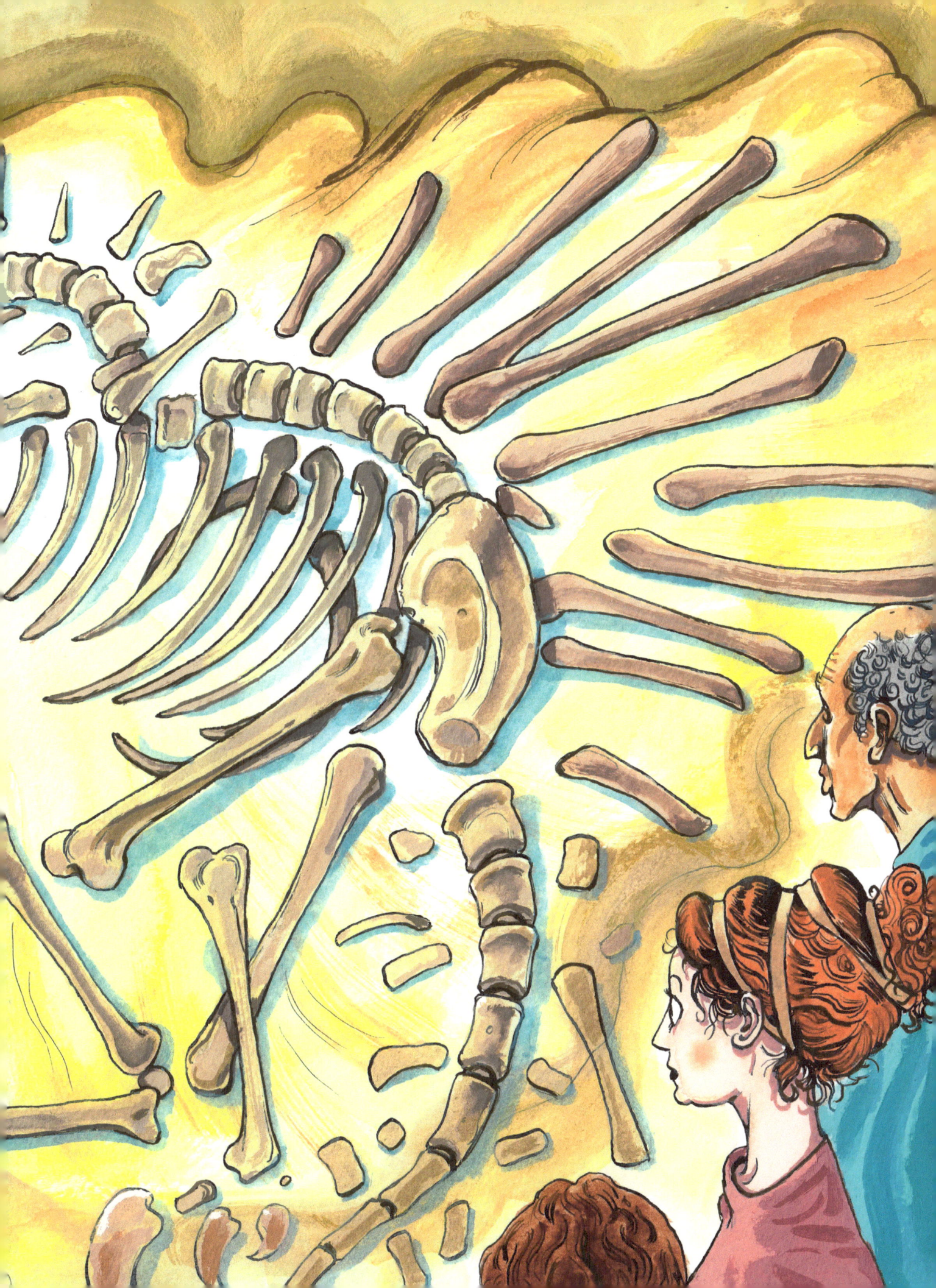

We had not heard Cleopatra Selene approach because of the rumpus, but she snatched us up and hid us among the folds of her costume.

"How ridiculous!" I said to Felix. "I hope they manage to put it back together properly for the Emperor's museum."

Words in this story with a Latin origin

English word......Latin word........Meaning

felix............felicis..........happy, lucky

triumph..........triumphus........achievement, success, procession

magnificent......magnificus.......splendid, great

canine...........canis............a dog

procession.......processio........to march forward

cauldron.........calidus..........hot

horrible.........horribilis.......horrendous, terrible

temple...........templum..........a building for worshipping god

vast.............vastus...........huge, immense

drape............drappus..........cloth

arena............arena............a sandy place

tepid............tepidus..........lukewarm

crocodile........crocodilus.......a crocodile

animal...........animalis.........an animal

FACT FILE

- A Triumph was a celebration, including a parade, in honour of a Roman leader who had won a victory over Rome's enemies. The enemy leaders, treasure and slaves were carried and lead through the city for everyone to see.

- On 15th August 29 BCE, Octavian had a Triumph celebrating his defeat of Queen Cleopatra in Egypt. He brought back her 11-year-old twins, Cleopatra Selene and Alexander Helios, who became orphans after the death of Cleopatra and their father, Mark Antony. The children were dressed as the sun and moon and walked with golden chains on them to show they had been captured.

- After the Triumph Octavian changed his name and became known as the Emperor Augustus Caesar.

- Isis was originally an ancient Egyptian goddess, but Romans worshipped many different gods and would often build new temples for deities from countries they had conquered.

- Roman baths had three sections: the warm tepidarium, the hot caldarium and finally the frigidarium with a cold water plunge bath.

- Food was often sold on the street from large heated pots, as many ordinary Romans lived in small apartments without kitchens.

- Laundries used urine to bleach white clothing, so were happy for donations of wee which they otherwise had to buy.

- Octavian had a museum of strange objects in his home on the Island of Capri. He was interested in ancient dinosaur bones and had some in his collection. Other Romans made grottos with displays of bones, although these were usually interpreted as Roman mythological creatures, monsters or giants.

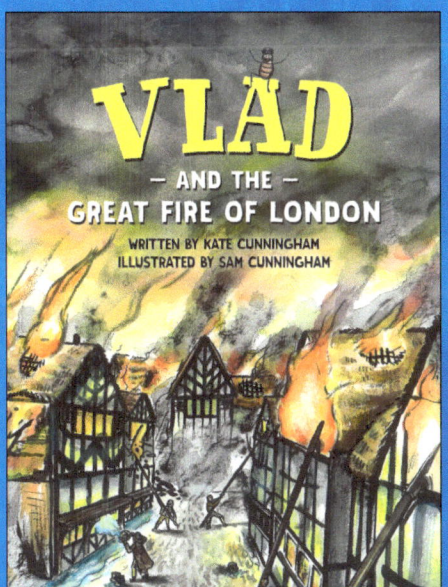
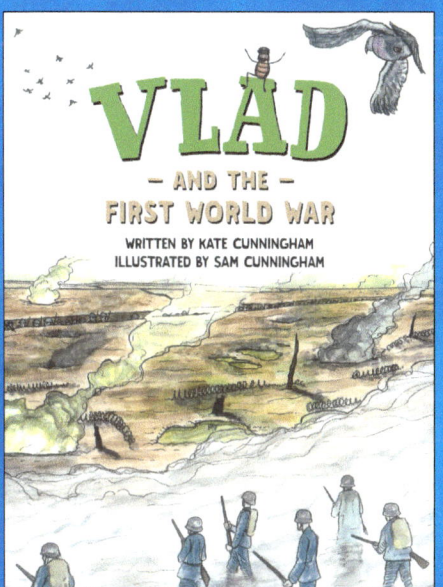
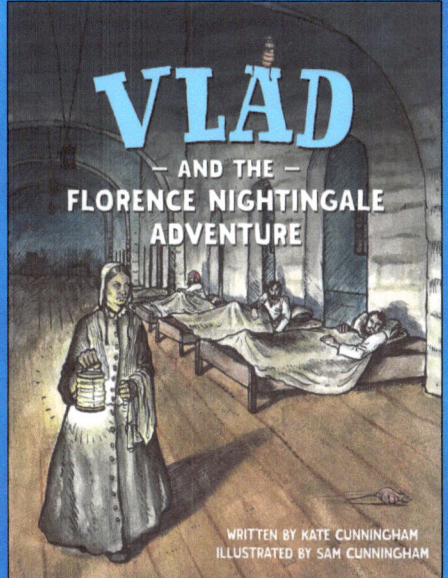
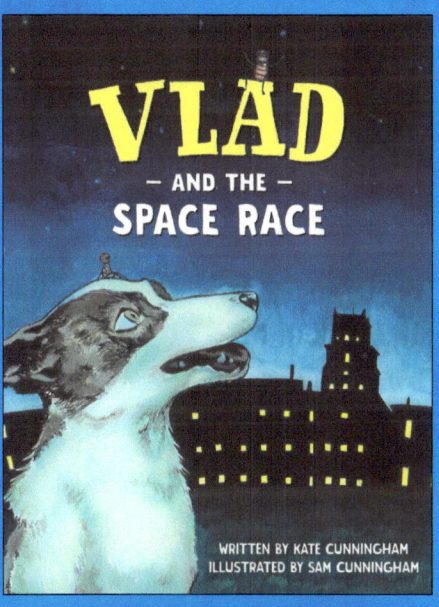
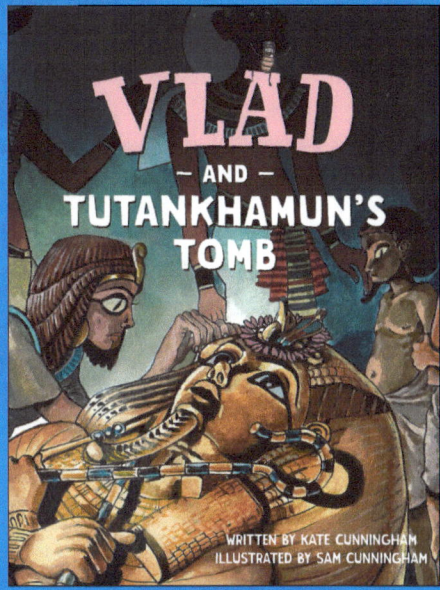

Also Available!

This is how big Vlad really is

Any errors are the responsibility of the author.

VLAD AND THE ROMAN TRIUMPH

Written by Kate Cunningham

Illustrated by Sam Cunningham

This paperback edition published 2022 by Reading Riddle

This edition designed by Rachel Lawston, lawstondesign.com

ISBN: 978-1-913338-14-5

Text copyright © Kate Cunningham

Illustrations copyright © Sam Cunningham

The right of Kate and Sam Cunningham to be identified as the Author and Illustrator of this work has been asserted by them in accordance with the Copyright Designs and Patents Act 1988.

All rights reserved.

For more information about Vlad flea, including games and free downloads, go to www.readingriddle.co.uk

www.ingramcontent.com/pod-product-compliance
Lightning Source LLC
Chambersburg PA
CBHW050758110526
44588CB00002B/45